A PORTRAIT OF LEEDS

A PORTRAIT OF LEEDS

JOHN MORRISON

HALSGROVE

First published in Great Britain in 2004

Title page: A show of colour in the formal gardens of Lotherton Hall.

British Library Cataloguing-in-Publication Data
A CIP record for this title is available from the British Library

ISBN 1 84114 378 2

HALSGROVE
Halsgrove House
Lower Moor Way
Tiverton, Devon EX16 6SS
Tel: 01884 243242
Fax: 01884 243325
email: sales@halsgrove.com
website: www.halsgrove.com

Printed and bound by D'Auria Industrie Grafiche Spa, Italy

Dedicated to Casey and Joe, solid Leeds citizens both.

Introduction

It was an unexpected pleasure to re-acquaint myself with Leeds. Born and raised in the city, I enjoyed visiting places I knew well, and discovering other places that, unforgivably, I knew nothing about at all. At the time I left Leeds it was a northern city with a world-beating football team, but whose most prosperous days seemed to belong to the past.

Leeds was promoting itself, bafflingly, as the 'Motorway City of the Seventies'. This modest slogan probably explains the coils of motorway flyovers and sliproads that came to occupy so much of South Leeds. The textile industries had helped to create the best and worst aspects of Leeds. With the industries' decline, the city floundered for a new role. But not for long.

It's amazing how quickly a city's fortunes can be reversed these days. Leeds has rebuilt itself, often in the most literal way. You will search in vain for much of Hunslet and Holbeck, south of the River Aire. It wasn't just the streets of red-brick, back-to-back houses that fell to the wrecking ball; whole postal districts were wiped off the map, to be replaced by industrial parks and housing estates. With the city embracing the service industries, there's less muck than there used to be, but, paradoxically, rather more brass. Now that the city's fortunes are on the rise, it's ironic that Leeds United FC has hit an unprecedented slump.

Young, urban professionals have taken to the delights of loft living, in the refurbished mills and warehouses that line the River Aire – having been persuaded that it's chic to live overlooking a river whose role, for the last two centuries, has been as an open sewer. London clubbers take the train up to Leeds, to enjoy the city's celebrated nightlife. Leeds' transformation into a shoppers' paradise was rubber-stamped, in 1996, when a branch of Harvey Nichols opened on Briggate.

This book represents a personal view of Leeds. And by 'Leeds', I mean not just the city itself, but the whole borough – which extends from the Wharfe Valley in the north, to the M62 motorway that slices through the South Pennine hills. To the east the borough borders the Vale of York, and includes sleepy villages such as Clifford and Boston Spa, whose cottages of gleaming limestone provide such a contrast to the red-brick terraces of Leeds.

To the west the city rubs up against neighboroughing Bradford – with barely an open field to separate these two, contrasting northern cities. The least celebrated part of the borough – the former coalfields to the south-east of Leeds – may be appreciated more in a few years, once the scars of mining have healed up. It may become known, with good reason, as Yorkshire's Lake District.

John Morrison
john@trunorth.demon.co.uk

Early morning by the River Aire, in the heart of the new riverside development, with the water as still as a millpond.

What a find, just outside Aberford, at the eastern extremity of the borough: the Gascoigne Almshouses, built in 1844 from gleaming limestone to house eight elderly residents.

Temple Newsham House, 'the Hampton Court of the North,' enjoys an enviable position – overlooking 1500 acres of parkland landscaped by Lancelot 'Capability' Brown.

Many a romantic rendezvous has begun beneath Dyson's Clock, a much-loved landmark on Lower Briggate.

As with Dyson's Clock, you have to lift your eyes beyond the modern shopfronts to see some fine architectural details.

St Paul's House, overlooking Park Square.

Atlas House in King Street.

Rooflines in Lower Briggate.

Though Park Square is the best-known square in Leeds, Queen Square, smaller and tucked away behind the Merrion Centre, has perhaps more charm.

There are very few half-timbered buildings around Leeds. This example – the Nookin – dates from 1611 and can be found near Oulton.

The Moravians, hailing from Bohemia, belonged to a Protestant episcopal church. They built Fulneck, during the middle of the eighteenth century, on an escarpment overlooking a wooded valley near Pudsey.

This decorative entrance to Armley Library is quite a contrast to the rest of the building, built in the red brick that's more typical of this area of Leeds.

For architectural inspiration, a lot of mill-owners looked to the east. Walk up Marshall Street, in Holbeck, to find Temple Mill – a surreal re-creation of the temple at Karnak in Egypt.

Old stonework is reflected in new windows at the Bourse, a courtyard off Boar Lane.

A statue of a lady with varicose vein problems, against the Georgian façades of Park Lane: once prestigious homes for well-heeled residents, now equally prestigious business addresses.

Joseph Priestley, renowned physicist and table tennis champion: one of the many bronze statues peopling City Square.

Bramham Park, an austere house on the opposite side of the A1 from Bramham village, is the venue every year for the Bramham Horse Trials.

Grassy avenues radiate from Bramham Park, like spokes on a wheel, offering vistas of tall hedges, water gardens and a selection of statues, pavilions and gazebos.

Harewood House, one of the self-proclaimed 'Treasure Houses of England', was built with money made by the Lascelles family in the West Indies from sugar and the slave trade.

In contrast to the Palladian pile that is Harewood House, a pair of cherubs frolic in a corner of the formal gardens.

Trees burst into blossom in Potternewton Park – revealing the candyfloss colours of spring.

Once a hunting ground, Roundhay Park was bought in 1872 for the people of Leeds. It is the perfect place, in high summer, for activities both energetic and sedentary.

Compared to the vainglorious monumentality of Harewood House, Edwardian Lotherton Hall, near Aberford, is an unpretentious family home.

The gardens of Lotherton Hall are on an intimate scale – matching the house itself – and are all the better for it.

A milestone in Bramhope – redolent of a time when travellers had time to stop and read a long list of possible destinations, graded in furlongs as well as miles.

When I was a lad, my dad took me to see this stone, standing near the entrance to Leeds-Bradford Airport. 'From this stone,' he said, portentously, 'you can get to anywhere in the world.' '*Anywhere,* dad?' 'Anywhere, son.' It was a moment of youthful epiphany.

An elaborate guide-stone on Kirkstall Road, celebrating the fact that Leeds lies halfway between London and Edinburgh.

A tranquil summer evening at Gott's Park – named for Leeds industrialist Benjamin Gott, who founded nearby Armley Mills.

Woodhouse Moor, close to the university, is a good place to relax with a book.

Streets of red-brick terraced houses, typical of many parts of Leeds, are becoming less typical with every year that passes.

The penny-plain exterior of a terraced house on Beeston Hill has been enlivened by a touch of floral colour.

The Garden Gate pub, now marooned in a housing estate in Hunslet, is an Edwardian gem.
The front is faced with high-glazed tiles that glow in the evening sunshine.

Even first-time visitors to the Albion pub, in Armley, may find it strangely familiar. For years the cardboard 'city pub' used with model railway layouts was based on it.

Thomas Chippendale, Otley's most famous son, won renown for his furniture. Fine examples can be seen at Harewood House and Temple Newsham House.

Next to the statue of Thomas Chippendale, in Manor Square, Otley, is the old Grammar School, founded in 1611, where he was a pupil.

God Loves Solicitors: a questionable statement at best.

The Leeds University campus expanded rapidly during the 1960s, when concrete was king.
Breezy concourse or windswept wasteland? The choice is yours.

Sixties concrete reflected in Nineties glass, above the shop-fronts of Bond Street.

Birds of indeterminate provenance sit on their perches and watch the to-ings and fro-ings of people in City Square.

A pair of hands extended in sculptured supplication: one of the many new additions to Millennium Square.

Dusk comes to Victoria Square, making silhouettes from the war memorial and the Town Hall dome.

This elaborate mural dominates a building close to Kirkgate Market.

A train pulls into Leeds Station, and a bus drives up Kirkgate: a busy scene overlooked by Leeds Parish Church.

The Royal Armouries, built in 1996 on one side of Clarence Dock, has had mixed fortunes in attracting visitors. Of course, once you've seen one bayonet, you've seen them all.

Clarence Dock, once a major component of the city's industrial past, is being reinvented as an upmarket 'urban village'.

Storm clouds gather over Thwaite Mill, a water-powered mill wedged between the River Aire and the Aire and Calder Navigation.

At any one moment, whole swathes of Leeds are a building site: a side-effect of the city's new-found wealth. This is the continued redevelopment of Millennium Square.

An inspired collage created by a fan of low-tar cigarettes.

A study in brick, wood and cast iron, beneath the arch of a railway viaduct.

A shower of rain invigorates the gardens of Lotherton Hall.

St John's Gardens, wedged between Merrion Street and St John's Church, is a haven for office workers who want a bit of time to themselves.

Wool traders used to gather in the Assembly Rooms, behind the Corn Exchange; now this handsome building offers alfresco dining.

Leeds has taken enthusiastically to a Mediterranean-style café life – despite the lack, for most of the year, of a Mediterranean-style climate.

A full house at Headingley Cricket Ground, to watch England being trounced, yet again, by the Aussies.

On market day in Otley, the stalls overflow the cobbled market place and extend the length of Kirkgate.

Millennium Square was crowded with overly optimistic England fans for Euro 2004, to watch the team lose on penalties. Again.

City Square at night – with the statue of the Black Prince floodlit against the facade of Queen's Hotel.

Kirkgate Market was rebuilt and extended, after a disastrous fire in 1975, with stalls spilling outside the main building.

In a city of smart new shops, fancy bistros and designer labels, people with more sense than money will still find bargains at Kirkgate Market.

Built during the 1620s by financier Sir Arthur Ingram – but now belonging to the city of Leeds – Temple Newsham House boasts pleasant waterside gardens.

This row of terraced houses has an enviable view – across Wharfemeadows Park, Otley, and the river itself.

The fair still comes each year to Woodhouse Moor, as it has done for generations, bringing light, colour and musical cacaphony.

Even with the competing attractions of computer games, there's still nothing as exhilarating (or stomach churning) as a ride on the waltzer.

Rolling countryside to the east of the borough, near Ledsham, just before the combine harvesters move in.

Night descends over the Wharfe Valley, near Harewood, with the setting sun like a red rubber ball.

Arthington Nunnery, built in 1585, is a handsome and unusual house with three rows of mullioned windows.

Thorner.

Ledsham.

To the north and east of Leeds are a number of picturesque villages that seem a long way from the bustle of Leeds.

A squadron of ducks, in strict formation, on the Leeds-Liverpool Canal at Rodley.

The canal basin at Granary Wharfe is another area of central Leeds that has had a major facelift. Where bargees once unloaded goods, people now relax.

My own tastes in architecture veer towards the vernacular: modest and unassuming buildings such as this neat little house in Bramhope.

The elliptical Corn Exchange, dating from 1861, was designed by Cuthbert Brodrick.
The 59 offices, surrounding the vast hall, now have a new lease of life as speciality shops.

Before pedestrianised streets came into vogue, the arcades of Leeds offered window shopping no matter what the weather.

The Grand Theatre, on Upper Briggate: seating for 2600 people in an auditorium of Victorian opulence.

The Jubilee Clock, erected in 1888 to commemorate Queen Victoria's Golden Jubilee, rises up behind the stalls in Otley's market square.

Just four communities within the borough of Leeds boast their own town halls. Leeds, of course, plus Wetherby, and, left, the tower of Morley Town Hall; on the right is Yeadon.

When Kirkstall Abbey was built – in 1152, by monks of the Cistercian order – it occupied a tranquil location next to the River Aire.

The city's industrial past has blackened the ruins of Kirkstall Abbey with smoke. Yet enough of the monastic compound remains, to reveal the rigours of monastic life in twelfth-century Yorkshire.

The village of Harewood was designed by John Carr of York. The houses, which share a unity of architectural style, line the long, straight avenue that leads to Harewood House itself.

It was the finding of sulphurous spring-water that transformed Boston Spa
from a mere village into a rather grand little town.

The Church of St John the Evangelist on New Briggate, dating from 1634, offers tranquility amid the bustle of city life.

It's not often that the River Aire looks this good – made molten by the reflections of the setting sun.

Leeds Town Hall, finished in 1858, speaks eloquently of a Victorian self-confidence. At the time that Cuthbert Brodrick submitted his plans, the city's place in the industrial landscape must have seemed secure.

The market town of Otley, and the Wharfe Valley that surrounds it, viewed from the rocky escarpment known as The Chevin.

Bramhope, one of the city's more prosperous suburbs, is just the place to build a home that would not have looked out of place on the film-set of *Dallas*.

A few doors away in Bramhope, but with more modest aspirations, is this charming little cottage.

Thorner, a few miles to the east of the city, is the sort of place where the wage-slaves of Leeds aspire to live.

A quiet corner of Clifford, another village that's been adopted by well-heeled commuters who spend their working days in the city.

Night – and a threatening storm cloud – descends on the rocks of The Chevin, near Otley.

A combination of mist and evening sunlight makes a dreamscape out of Woodhouse Moor and its rows of leafless trees.

Middleton Railway, in South Leeds, claims to be the oldest working railway in the world. When it was built, in 1758, the colliery wagons were drawn by horses.

The Middleton Railway is popular with fans of very short rail journeys. Travellers are shunted by steam loco into Middleton Woods and then, soon after, shunted back.

The working days are over for this steam engine at Middleton Railway.

The Dortmund Drayman, a statue erected in 1980 to mark the twinning of Leeds with another city – Dortmund in Germany – that's famous for its beer.

The Inner Ring Road surrounds the centre of the city like a tarmacadam tourniquet.

Though not the biggest of football fans, I can still name most of Don Revie's great team of the 1970s. Unlike the members of the current team who ply their trade at Elland Road.

Golden Acre, near Bramhope, is one of the most delightful of the city's parks.
Back in the 1930s it was a miniature Alton Towers; now it's a haven for wildlife.

Halcyon days on the Leeds-Liverpool Canal near Rodley, where the waterway presents a more rural aspect.

Early morning at Granary Wharf canal basin: another once-forgotten part of the city that has had a much-needed facelift.

There's something about canals and narrowboats that brings a smile to peoples' faces. Maybe that's because it's the last technology that everyone can understand.

Centenary Footbridge, the most recent bridge to be built over the River Aire, in 1993.

In one of the city's favourite rags-to-riches stories, Harry Ramsden started frying fish and chips in a wooden hut in Guiseley. Now it's a worldwide franchise.

Wharfemeadows Park, in Otley, offers riverside walks, ducks to feed and, in summer, dinghies to row.

Another view of the River Wharfe – and the weir that helped to divert water into the old corn mill – at Wetherby, from the old bridge.

A statue of a smiling Billy Bremner stands outside Elland Road, to remind long-suffering fans of a time when Leeds United were indisputably the best team in the land.

Nearly as frightening as Billy Bremner going into a tackle, this grotesque face – based on a mask given to King Henry VIII – is now the logo of the Royal Armouries.

Leeds City Art Gallery and a Reclining Nude by Henry Moore, one of West Yorkshire's most famous sons.

A statue in City Square of John Harrison, one of the city's most prominent benefactors. Giving him a glass to hold is the sort of thing that students get up to, once the pubs have closed.

A pastoral view across the suburbs of West Leeds, from Farnley.

Golfers play a round in Gotts Park – given to the city by industrialist Benjamin Gott – with the terraced houses of Burley as a backdrop.

This building was once the entrance to the White Cloth Hall, where pieces of locally produced cloth were bought and sold; now it's a restaurant.

One of the city's most elegant Georgian houses, at number 18, Park Street.

There are some surprising rural spots close to the city. Cars rush by on the nearby ring road, leaving the canal, here at Rodley, to kids and their fishing nets.

Old commercial buildings rub shoulders with new, to create a residential complex overlooking the River Aire.

Dial House, in Halton – a handsome and sternly symmetrical house, built of brick with stone dressings.

High-rise flats can be dressed up with colourful balconies, but the truth is self-evident: high-rise living was a social experiment which failed.

The Parkinson Building, the public face of the university campus, is unusual – for Leeds, at least – in being faced with white Portand stone.

This mosque, in the Hyde Park area of the city, is a sign of changing times. Despite the minarets, it doesn't look out of place among the red-brick terraces which surround it.

The diminutive Church of St John the Baptist, tucked away in the suburb of Adel, is sought out by lovers of old churches – particularly for the carved Norman arches which surround the door.

The Church of All Hallows, in Bardsey, is like a time capsule of architectural styles. The small Anglo-Saxon building was extended over a thousand years to meet the needs of larger congregations.

New riverside developments provide a congenial working environment for many of the new businesses springing up in Leeds.

If you see a fish jump, from the less-than-limpid waters of the River Aire, it's probably just trying to catch its breath.

Tower Works, on Globe Road, boasts two intriguing architectural features. The chimney in the background was based on a belltower in Verona; the dust-extraction shaft re-creates, in red brick, Giotto's Campanile in Florence.

When the Headrow was pedestrianised, years ago, it was dubbed 'The Hedgerow'. Today it is a bus-only route through the heart of the city.

The Civic Hall, another confection in white Portland stone, is a surprisingly recent addition to the Leeds skyline – having been built in 1933.

One of the art nouveau statues in City Square – some called 'Morn', others 'Even' – silhouetted against new office buildings.

Rows of terraced houses in Kirkstall descend steeply to Kirkstall Road and the Aire Valley.

Rows of red-brick houses are named to form distinct communities: here can be found Harold Street, Harold View, Harold Walk, Harold Mount, Harold Grove and Harold Avenue.

The tower of St Peter's, the Parish Church of Leeds, rises head-and-shoulders above a block of riverside apartments.

The Saxon Church of All Saints, in pale stone, dominates the village of Ledsham. Not just architecturally, either; even today the village pub is closed on Sundays.

Another view of the Centenary Bridge across the Aire, and a smart riverside restaurant.

Rowers being put through their paces on the River Aire, in the centre of Leeds.

This statue of Queen Victoria stood outside the Town Hall until 1937, when it was relegated to a corner of Woodhouse Moor.

Under stormy skies a swan swims across the main lake at Fairburn Ings – a nationally famous bird reserve now looked after by the RSPB.

The Chevin Forest Park – 700 acres of woodland, heath and gritstone crags, overlooking the Wharfe Valley – is where the residents of North Leeds go to stretch their legs.

Adel Woods form part of a wedge of parkland – including the Hollies and Meanwood Park – which extends almost into the heart of the city.

Cars and pedestrians make an uneasy mix, now that the York Road slices unsympathetically through communities to the east of Leeds.

Leeds Bridge House, with its cast iron frame and unusual triangular shape, wouldn't look out of place in New York or Chicago.

City Square has undergone a number of face-lifts over the last century – from roundabout to its present incarnation as a public space for pedestrians.

Vicar Lane and the city's Victorian Quarter, with a glass canopy creating another all-weather arcade of fashionable shops.

Fairburn Ings is merely the best-known of many stretches of water in the south-east corner of the borough – created from old colliery workings and slowly going 'back to Nature'.

Beyond the rolling pastures in front of Temple Newsham House are gardens with good shows of rhododendrons.

The sun sets on Knotford Nook, a small expanse of water between Pool and Otley, where ducks dabble and fishermen try their luck.